The HERO Method

A Powerful Job Hunting Tool for Veterans:

By **George Valentine**

Table of Contents:

Introduction:

How HERO helps you in the Hunt

The Employer's Point of View

Making It Work: Worksheets on the Employer's Perspective

You Are More Than You Think You Are

Making It Work: YOUR HERO Skills

The Employer's Language

Making It Work: Putting In The Right Words:

Putting It All To Work: Tips for YOUR HERO victory

Introduction:

Character and drive are two qualities that employers search for – the qualities that could remain largely under the surface in your resume, applications and job interview preparations but are part of who you are and would show themselves I n work each day.

As a veteran this is not news to you, it is part of what you have already developed in your service. Through the HERO Method, you will learn the four basics of every job that ever was or ever will be, how to better skills appreciate your qualities and the needs for potential employers in each of these basic areas.

In this short book, I am introducing you to a powerful, unique way to bring new strength to your job hunting. The HERO Method is a way that especially you as a veteran can have more in your job hunt.
HERO shows you in quick, direct and easy ways to learn, use and teach the method to others.

Veterans of the military face three important challenges that others looking for work largely do not. The HERO Method solves each of them.

1. Many employers do not know how to relate the work you have done and skills you have developed to the demands of their work. You can now do that connecting for them.
2. Many skills you have developed do not fit easily on a current resume format.
3. Employers use language different from one you have become used to.

The HERO Method helps you learn the four basics of every job and assists you in understanding the employer's point of view on each of them. It also helps you learn about yourself and how to express that you have the qualities the employers are looking for.

Happy hunting!

1. How the HERO Method Helps YOU.

The Job Hunting HERO Method Based on three basic principles:
- **understand any employer's POV**
	If you do not understand the employer's Point of View (POV), you will leave the interview as you arrived, unemployed. Most job hunters never take the time to learn and appreciate the point of view (POV) of the employer, the one person who's opinion in the job interview maters. Maybe they research the company applied to or the job duties of the new placement, but it is essential to see the job in the employer's eyes. HERO gives you an effective road map for your job hunting.

- **understand your own own hidden strengths**

You have strengths that do not easily make their way to your resume, applications and interview preparation – until now. Veterans have a special need in this area as employers may not have a true understanding of just what you have done or can grow to accomplish in the future.

- **be able to tell of these strengths in a way the employer appreciates.**

You need to be able to express your strengths in a way that employers can understand addresses their needs and concerns. Just as years ago Chevy had problems selling the Nova in Mexico until they noted that No-va in Spanish means won't go and that no one wanted to buy a car called the "won't go" you need to appreciate the language of your audience, the employers.

2. Every job needs a HERO – Seeing the Employer's POV

Every job that ever was or ever will be requires the four special aspects of the HERO method. Here we look at the world from the employer's point of view.

- I need someone with the **heart** to treat my customers as they expect to be treated, other staff as they need to get along and supervisors how they will need to be treated.
- Someone who maintains focus and **energy** on the job and sees it through no matter their personal issues such as stress or physical concerns.
- Someone who can **relearn** what they need to understand about the job and have the ability to learn and adapt to changes as they will inevitably occur.
- A new staffer who will **own the work that they do** and take responsibility for it.

Let us look deeper into the four essentials:

Heart: The employer is concerned: can each person selected for jobs address the needs and expectations of clients; can she be integrated smoothly into the employer's team and will not hurt the agency with the other people and groups related to their work.

Clients -

Show the employer that you can see the world from another person's perspective. Can you appreciate their needs, expectations, concerns of how they want to be treated by the employer? Show that you can appreciate the world from our client's point of view generally and that you have significant experience in that world.

Remember that the employer is keeping in mind two things:

A. Hey, my name is on the building – my reputation is on the line because of whom I surround myself with among my employees. If you treat my customers badly and do not meet their expectations and concerns, they will remember ME a lot longer than they remember YOU.

B. I know that one complaint against my business cancels out 10 compliments. With social media so much an important part of day to day with the ability to effect public perceptions of the company image, any employee, especially a new one, has the ability to hurt my company.

I just want to avoid buyers remorse of "why did I hire THIS person?"

Co-workers and supervisors-

There are norms in how the staff relates to each other – when a new staffer joins in, there is a shake up or 'storm' in that relationship. My concern is keeping the storm from effecting company operations.

In daily operations and in inevitable changes that will occur, interactions between staff will change – can I be sure that you will not be a problem in keeping things moving forward well. Can you appreciate their expectations of you on the job?

Are you able to hear me and understand my intentions about doing the job - I need you to do it so I can walk away and know you are doing it 'the right way'? That we will get along and you will not work against what I need you to do?

E: Energy Do YOU have **the focus and energy** for the job?

Employers need to know beyond a doubt that you can retain the focus you need to do the job consistently right. Can you meet the needs of the job – focus and energy – whether you are having a good day or a bad one? Will you be just as motivated and on-task at the end of the day than you are at the start?

I can't have your mind wandering too much – you need to be focused on the work and the needs of clients and co-workers. Sure, everyone has life pressures, distractions and aches and pains, but will they take a toll on your work ethic and practice? Can I walk away from you at any time during the work day knowing your quality of work stays consistently solid?

R: Relearning. Can you **learn the job and adapt** to changes as they arise?

People normally do not have the specific education and training to step in on the first day and do the job the way the employer wants it done. Whether it is using transferable skills, adjusting to new software or learning how the new boss wants it done, there is learning and re-learning to be done.

Can you show that you have the capability to learn efficiently and to adapt as circumstances change? Can you learn efficiently?

No matter what you have done in the past, you will need to effectively learn the way that we do things. Your educational background may help, but you will need to learn efficiently so we can allow you to work independently and address problems as they arise... and they will arise.

As you learn about the job, there will be changes going on and you will need to adapt to the changes. It is a lot to understand about you and your capabilities... can you show me you have those skills?

O: Owning   Being conscientious and responsible for the work you do.
Do you **take ownership** of your work?

Everyone makes mistakes, but the employer needs to know that you will learn from constructive criticism of the times you do not get it right. Owning the work you do includes taking pride in the work that has YOUR name on it, work that shows you will take responsibility for wins and losses.

Even the most intelligent, hardest working person who cares about our clients will be washed out if he does not grow from his mistakes. We need someone who will accept blame for mistakes and grow from them and will also revel in the times he gets it right.

Making It Work – Employer POV:

Now we take time and space for writing your answers to each of the HERO, employer POV questions for the top four employer opportunities that you have right now.

Keep these sheets as we will be returning to them later. Remember, answer from what you consider the employer's point of view:

HEART:

We relate to our clients in a special way. How would you express that kind of way of relating?

1. _____
2. _____
3. _____
4. _____

Do you have experience in dealing with people in that 'way of relating'?

1. _____
2. _____
3. _____
4. _____

Staff interact in a way that promotes our effective and efficient work – do you have experience in that kind of work with others?

1. _____
2. _____
3. _____
4. _____

ENERGY:
Give me examples of how you have been able to keep your focus in tough or stressful situations.

1. _____
2. _____
3. _____
4. _____

__Having Drive__ means you actively go after work that others may not do – like the waitress who clears tables overseen by other wait staff because it is the right thing to do, or the retail clerk who runs outside in the rain and brings in shopping carts from the parking lot without being asked. "Drive" is a valuable quality for any staff – but largely is part of a person's personality and cannot be taught or enforced.

Do you have drive? Give three examples that show that you have used your drive when others may not have done what you have done.

1. _____
2. _____
3. _____
4. _____

RELEARNING:
Describe three things that you had to learn well quickly.

1. _____

2. _____

3. _____

4. _____

How did you know, in those examples, when you had learned it?

1. _____

2. _____

3. _____

4. _____

Give two examples of your having to adapt to change such as in learning (such as a computer program), actions (such as new procedures) or responsibilities (such as job duties).

1. _____

2. _____

3. _____

4. _____

OWNING THE WORK YOU DO:

When did you take responsibility when avoiding it would have been easier for you? What was the impact on you?

1._____

2._____

3._____

4._____

Detail two examples of errors you had made; what you learned from the experience and how you changed for how you faced things in the future.

1._____

2._____

3._____

4._____

Describe how it feels when you have given constructive criticism to others.

1._____

2._____

3._____

4._____

YOU ARE MORE THAN YOU THINK YOU ARE

Divergent thought worksheet to understand what you have to offer.

"Divergent thought", thinking in broad terms about building a list of what you have done in the past and can do in the future.

Hidden skills.
Heart:
Relating with others, ability to coordinate well with others toward a shared goal.

As a veteran, you have had to work with others in stressful situations and prove time and again that you have what it takes to understand their perspective. Consider who your clients were, whether helping in a community or upholding the reputation of the armed services in the town you lived, you have expressed an understanding of knowing the client's point of view.

Energy:
Strength in your abilities to focus and to have energy, from start to end of the day.

Though it is plain to you that you have proven several times to your superiors your capability to be focused and energized through the long and varied hours you have worked, the civilian employer may not know it well. You need to use employer's language expressing that you have this quality.

Relearning:
Ability to learn and adapt to changes in responsibilities, processes, information.

Throughout your career, you have had to adapt many times to new technology, new instructions and you have proven your ability to listen, learn and act effectively on what you have learned. Wherever the job hunt takes you there will be the task of building on the information you already have learned. NOW show your skills in learning and adapting in a new environment.

Owning :
Taking responsibility for your work and growing from correction.

In the military, more than many other fields, you gain both a sense of responsibility/pride in work you do. From the first days of boot camp, you have built on that understanding and when you can prove this to a prospective employer, you are well on your way to answering the toughest of the four essentials to any job.

Our next step is for you to prove first to yourself the skills and HERO qualities you already have. Now we focus on the divergent thought worksheets about what makes you so special.

Making It Work: Learning of Your Personal Strengths

HEART:

Give four examples of how you have dealt with or learned the expectations of people different from yourself. (ex. Cared for a disabled relative; worked in a day care center, successful in sales)

1. _____
2. _____
3. _____
4. _____

What is hardest part for you in providing services/coping with the people like those you would deal with on the job you want? Give examples:

1. _____
2. _____
3. _____
4. _____

Give examples of how you deal with difficult co-workers.

1. _____
2. _____
3. _____

What would your co-worker references say about your ability to work well with others?

1. _____
2. _____
3. _____

What are the aspects of your work and life experience that build on your HERO qualities?

In more detail:
How would you describe your clients/co-workers, supervisors in four different situations (jobs, volunteering, life situations)?

1. _____
2. _____
3. _____
4. _____

What was their perspective, what did they need for you to understand in working with them.
- Dealing with the workload   * Timeliness   * Eye to detail   * Problem solving

1. _____
2. _____
3. _____
4. _____

How to show that you did right by them and met their needs/concerns?
- Coordination of the team * Anticipating change * Training Others
- Any other stakeholders?   What was the community served?

1. _____
2. _____
3. _____
4. _____

Making It Work: Learning of Your Personal Strengths

ENERGY:

Three examples of your putting in effort and drive in work or life situations (ex. Working unexpected overtime, being in athletics, helping others when not asked, community involvement).

1. _____
2. _____
3. _____

Three examples of how you deal with unexpected demands.

1. _____
2. _____
3. _____

How do you maintain your focus on tasks when under stress? (Late night studies, multi-tasking)

_____

Give four examples of what you have accomplished while under stress.

1. _____
2. _____
3. _____
4. _____

In More Detail:

Examples of how you have been able to keeping focus, energy – ways you may use in your next job.

1. _____
2. _____
3. _____
4. _____

Describe how you maintain your focus : Beating distractions
- mental toughness   * extra shifts, unexpected overtime
- were you no different on a good day from bad day.

1._____

2. _____

3. _____

4._____

Making It Work: Learning of Your Personal Strengths
RELEARNING:

Give examples of something you have learned when you were under pressure to learn for life/work obligations. (Caring for medical needs of another, operation of machinery)

1. _____
2. _____
3. _____
4. _____

How will your learning skills be helpful at your new job? Give three examples:

1. _____
2. _____
3. _____

Give examples of your successfully adapting to change (things, actions).

1. _____
2. _____
3. _____
4. _____

In More Detail:
R: Learning and adapting in examples at work/life
- use of technology   * examples of learning/applying something quickly
     * information management   *dealing with changes working with people/things

How do you know when you have learned or adapted effectively?

1. _____
2. _____
3. _____
4. _____

Making It Work: Learning of Your Personal Strengths

OWNING THE WORK YOU DO:
Give examples of times you took responsibilities for actions both positive and negative.

1. _____
2. _____
3. _____
4. _____

Give examples of how you have grown and changed from correcting your errors and growing from constructive criticism you have received.

1. _____
2. _____
3. _____
4. _____

In More Detail:
O: Challenges faced and errors made.
When you have had the opportunity to take responsibility and leadership, do you?

1. _____
2. _____
3. _____

When you are given conflicting orders how do react?

1. _____
2. _____
3. _____

The Janitor Game

One way to appreciate you are more than you think you are is to get together with people for what I have learned to call: The Janitor Game.

Early on I learned that job hunters often assume using the title of a job they have held is enough for an introduction to a prospective employer – this is not so and I proved it myself – the hard way.

Years ago I was asked to hire a person to work in a temp job as a janitor – easy assignment, right? I found someone who stated he had years of experience as a "janitor", so I hired him.

An hour into the job I got a call from his supervisor asking to fire him and hire someone else quickly. What happened was that the person I sent was given a buffing machine which was tossing my employee around the room, causing other workers to fall down laughing and causing chaos in getting work done.

I quickly found another person for the job, but I learned that sometimes what an employer thinks a job title means may not tell the whole story. It may cause a lot of laughter, but even that is never good.

So I created the Janitor Game for you to learn from my mistake. Here is how it goes:

Get a few people together and tell them JUST THE TITLE of a job you have held and ask them to list five responsibilities that they believe you would have had in that job.

At the same time, privately list for yourself of fifteen duties you had from the start to the end of a average day. If you would like, make another list of the range of responsibilities you had from when you started the job to today to show how they had evolved.

When you compare their lists with yours, you can see how someone with little information other than the title will make guesses and will miss points of your skills and experience you want your prospective employer to know about you.

Use these pages to practice writing bullets describing your skills/qualifications for resume, application and interview preparation.

HEART:

ENERGY:

Use these pages to practice writing bullets describing your skills/ qualifications for resume, application and interview preparation.

RELEARNING:

OWNING:

Connecting Your Language with the Employer's

You have an understanding of what the employer is looking for in the four essentials of the job and have a better understanding of your own hidden skills in each of these four areas. Now we wrap it all together making the connections between what you have to say and the way that the employer is listening.

It is important that you use action words in the past tense showing that you have gained the essential skills in each of the four areas, but you need to connect to their needs for the specific jobs:

Return to your list of the four top prospects you have for landing the job you are seeking. **Consider the action words, description of your experiences and skills at each question, noting it will be different for each of the four employers.**

HEART:
Dealing with clients:
What is the nature of the interaction with clients? (Collaboration, motivation, negotiation? What needs did you address?)

Can you describe their expectations in working with the employer's agency? (Problem solving? Investigation, **research**, consistency? What qualified as a positive interaction?)

1. _____

2. _____

3. _____

Is there a repetition in the way the clients are treated, such as a cashier? What is your experience with that kind of consistent repetition?

What have you done to gain or maintain 'customers' for the employer?

Describe the level of intimacy the employee has in dealing with clients – from medical concerns to mundane topics. What is your experience with that level of connection?

Co-workers:
What is your experience working with others in the way this employer has – such as in creating a finished product; providing an on-going service or other 'product'?

1. _____

2. _____

3. _____

What level of independence do you work best in? What is the best style of management makes you most efficient and effective?

ENERGY:
Focus:
Discuss how you maintain concentration to task. What helps you the most in that role?

What are the challenges you face in maintaining focus if you landed this job?

How do you deal with repetition in the work you do? What is your self-care to avoid 'burnout'?

Physical energy:
Give examples of you how addressed unexpected demands such as overtime, sudden changes in deadlines.

1._____

2._____

3._____

How have you dealt with other physical challenges?

RE-LEARNING
Learning:
Give examples of how you have learned new processes and roles, (interacting with others), items (such as menu items) or activities (caring for others).

1._____

2._____

3._____

How do you know that you "got it" and could put what you had learned to practice? (Processed, coordinated, managed, etc.) Give examples of how to put what you have learned into practice, such as training, supervising others.

1._____

2._____

3._____

Adapt:
How did you recognize your need to adapt? (Anticipated, interacted with team members, collaborated, problem solved.)

Give examples of your adapting and problem solving as needed. (Interaction with supervisors, appreciating clients needs/concerns)

Explain some ways you will need to adapt yourself in the job you are applying for.

OWNING:
Growing from constructive criticism:
Describe criticisms and corrections you have received and how you have reacted from it. (personal weaknesses and how you have addressed them)

Give examples of something you have learned/changed through trial and error. (steps taken to address weaknesses, working well with supervisors)

1. _____

2. _____

3. _____

Conscientiousness:
Describe situations wherein you have expressed problems and addressed those issues at home or work. (School, work, community issues)

Give examples of your being responsible for both some good news and bad news in either your life or job (sports, family, employment).

1. _____

2. _____

3. _____

How do you deal with co-workers who are not as truthful and conscientious?

Putting It To Work: Ways to Remember and Utilize the HERO Method

Here are some videos which reinforce many of the concepts behind the HERO Method, enjoy!

Comparing Yourself To Buddy:
Here you gain a greater sense of what makes you special and your skills and qualities unique – at least compared to Buddy.
www:youtube.com/watch?v=0TXZIMt9HR8

Babe Ruth's Lesson
An important lesson in the Hunt from that poor fella, one of baseball's worst and then again most unlikely heroes– Babe Ruth.
www:youtube.com/watch?v=yaUt7K6stao

Cheeseburger Voice
Finding the right tone of voice when talking with the employer about how great you are – lessons from Johnny Uzzi.
www:youtube.com/watch?v=v5Mj_PB0rMk

Ending your answers with a Period
My first lesson in job hunting as a 7 year old dish dryer.
www:youtube.com/watch?v=UFtC0K2ybls

Sluggers: Don't do Job Hunting On The Cheap
Taking a lesson from Valentine's Dinner's baseball team.
www:youtube.com/watch?v=z_1_4mYelvg

Frosting versus cake
Where I get to perfect my evil laugh.
www:youtube.com/watch?v=hrEUs0cG_uQ

Don't "Use" References
Keeping your references from becoming, well, animals.
www:youtube.com/watch?v=C6koHLqal9M

www.ingramcontent.com/pod-product-compliance
Lightning Source LLC
Chambersburg PA
CBHW050039230526
45470CB00003B/1360